I0531614

BETWEEN
THE SPACES

OF

A WRITER'S LIFE

by

Shirley Ann Parker

BETWEEN THE SPACES OF A WRITER'S LIFE

Cover art and internal text Copyright © 2011 Shirley Ann Parker

All Rights Reserved. No part of this book may be reproduced in any form or by any electronic, mechanical, magnetic or photographic means, including the use of information storage and retrieval systems, without permission in writing from the copyright owner. Although every precaution has been taken in the preparation of this book, the publisher and author assume no responsibility for errors or omissions. Neither is any liability assumed for damages resulting from the use of the information contained herein.

www.shirleyannparker.com

ISBN 978-0-9720-8056-9

Published by:
Topaz Cove Creations
P.O. Box 4878, West Hills, CA 91308-4878
Fax: 818-716-7958
topazcove@hotmail.com

BETWEEN THE SPACES OF A WRITER'S LIFE

Table of Contents

Introduction

Between the Spaces collects just some of my personal reflections on the everyday human condition, at least as I have observed and experienced it in today's world. I have tried to retain my sense of humor where it is appropriate. However, so many individuals lie around like rocks, either expecting to be waited on hand and foot, and/or using their arrogance to annoy and bully others.

We have freedom of choice to be a parasite if we wish. Even so, there is a sad waste of human potential and a loss of good that could have resulted from such people applying themselves and their latent talents to doing something useful in this world, to paying their rent for the space they occupy on earth. Such losses are probably immeasurable.

It is for the rest of us to pay attention, to throw up an arm in our own defense, and to step in and fight for others where there is any hope of not making things worse for them. Even then, we are obligated to speak up or act in some way on their behalf. The smallest kind gesture can lift their spirits and give them the courage to go on.

Note that I have left the grand philosophizing to those who enjoy taking on something larger than windmills. It is the smaller aggravations and repeated insults that can wear us down and erode our self-esteem, like the abuse of wind and rain against canyon walls over many decades.

We deal with the ongoing maintenance chores of life, like grocery shopping, push back when someone does not give the proper service value, or worse, starts to act as if he or she owns us. Life is full of challenges and frustrations to be resolved. Sometimes we win outright. Sometimes we must wait for karma to catch up with the offenders. Retribution is the first law of the universe, after all. For every cause there is an effect. And should you have reason not to believe this now, just wait and see.

A Lone Voice Does Make a Difference

Occasionally there's little response to your postings on the Internet, and no interest at all shown by paper editors. Those may be the days when you feel you might be better off writing graffiti, instead of wasting your time on essays and articles. At least graffiti polluters get attention. Of course, it's invariably the wrong kind. Rare is the true artist who creates beautiful murals in the neighborhoods. I've always thought that if we could catch graffiti scribblers often enough, their punishment should be to clean up their own trash and everyone else's within a few square miles, and then do community service to learn how much more valuable and helpful they could be with their abilities, instead of destructive.

Now that I've digressed, does it ever seem that you can't make a difference in the world? What can one writer do in a world of loud-mouthed giants of varying talents? How can a single, lowborn voice be heard in a world dominated by the scions of the silver-spoon-in-the-mouth brigade? (Or the silver-foot-in-the-mouth troop!) What do you do when you're only one and small?

Someone once posed that same question to a mosquito. The pesky insect hardly stopped whining long enough to answer. "See that big guy over there?" (*whine*) "He thinks he's going to get a well-deserved nap." (*whine, whine*) "Watch me!" (*whine, whine, whine*). And you can fill in the rest of the story yourself. Anyone, regardless of size, can indeed make a difference in the world, even when he or she is perceived as something of a pest.

It doesn't matter how small you are, or how insignificant your co-workers or bosses deem you to be. Sooner or later, you will make your point, drive the nail home, or cause someone to become so uncomfortable that you bring about badly needed social change. It might even be in that corporate environment that is so filled with spite, or in a larger area of the real world. The corporate arena, in case you didn't know, isn't the real world. As a veteran of the business environment, I can state it's merely a stage where people play out their dramas, often at your expense. But at very least, it's free entertainment, though the wounds are real enough!

Never think your voice isn't worth hearing. You might need to check the ground under your feet and the condition of your bank account first, but always in a so-called free society, there is a reason to speak out, and a way to do so. When it comes to the Internet, praise the Lord, and pass the ammunition!

# # #

Camping In the Uinta Mountains

One of my most unforgettable short vacations was spent in the Uinta Mountains of Wasatch National Forest in Utah. In a state replete with spectacular scenery, the Uintas (named after one of the Ute Indian tribes of the region) are Utah's highest mountains and the only range in the nation to run east-west. While camping in the region, my husband and I laughed and cried, were frightened, frozen and enchanted.

Unable, at first, to make up our minds where to go camping in the state, we asked around, receiving almost as many different answers as people have outdoor interests. Finally, we decided on an area a fishing enthusiast had enjoyed. We didn't think to ask him when he had last camped in the area. Still, it was the second recommendation for this near-wilderness area, so that had influenced our decision positively.

Only much later did we also discover that no dyed-in-the-wool fisherman ever tells anyone where the good fishing is.

"Cold up there? In August? No, don't worry about it. You'll be fine!" a next-door neighbor told us.

You learn many things as novice campers, especially in an unfamiliar state. One is - never pay any attention to another person's definition of cold, especially if the individual is more well-padded than you are.

My sleeping bag, from a famous manufacturer, was guaranteed down to 32 degrees Fahrenheit, according to the salesman. I must admit he did not say what it was guaranteed to do, but my husband seemed to think the sleeping bag was supposed to keep me warm.

"Perfect," he said. "I'd never get her out camping in anything colder."

His generic sleeping bag was more heavy-duty than mine. Even so, we shivered most of that first night. We slept inside our tent on foam pads, fully-clothed inside the bags (except for boots and jackets), with a blanket and old comforter on top of that, and our coats over our feet. We hardly dared move for fear of finding another, even colder spot somewhere.

"Whose idea was this?" I muttered at one point, giving one of my loud shudders for which I am famous within our circle of family and close friends.

"Oh, it isn't that cold," objected my husband.

But it wasn't <u>my</u> knees I heard knocking together. A little later, I heard a suspicious chuckle from his direction and grinned in spite of myself. The whole scenario was ridiculous. August or not, night at 9,500' in the Uinta Mountains of northern Utah is cold.

I reflected on the drive to this rather remote spot. The state road (#072) that begins 7 miles south of Mountainview, Wyoming and leads to China Lake is about 15 miles of gravel or dirt, with some stretches of it designated as "primitive" on maps. It was traversable by compact car if the vehicle did not ride low to the ground and if such a car had a cautious driver. Four-wheel-drive was and likely still is a safer bet all around.

Eventually, of course, we did get comfortable enough to drift off to sleep, the kind of sound sleep that comes after fresh air, sunshine and a moderate amount of hiking around.

Next morning, we awakened to pitter-pattering on the roof. My first thought was "Oh no! Rain!" yet my eyelids were being assaulted by bright sunlight. The noise was being made by squeaky, cheeky chipmunks letting us know it was time to get up and get with it.

"Do you hear them?" I asked my husband.

He nodded and said, "There must be a whole family out there."

I crawled from one cocoon into another to venture outside. Wide awake now, I gasped in delight at our surroundings. The earliest rays of the sun smashed the black glass of the lake into a myriad of golden sparkles. I sat combing the tangles out of my hair while listening to the soft singing of the wind in the pines. A small fish took a free fly across the lake and the miniature plop of his return into the water could have happened two feet away, so distinct was it. After a brief hesitation, the chipmunks resumed their busyness and play. Grooming was something that did not seem to threaten them.

Our stomach grumbles disturbed the air, so before they got too loud, we prepared breakfast-- oatmeal and mugs of hot chocolate. The chipmunks vanished until we started eating. Then they returned, wild and shy. They had few visitors in this spot, compared to the improved campgrounds at China Meadows.

The chipmunks finally let their curiosity overcome their fear. One bounced up on to my left foot, crossed the other foot and dived into the cereal dish. I remained perfectly still as he lapped up the buttery milk with a tiny pink tongue. He tidied his whiskers and his chest, and then looked around for more enjoyment. Spotting the oatmeal-coated saucepan, he scampered over to that, pausing frequently to stir the air with his tail to make sure he wasn't headed for trouble.

A friend or relative arrived from the other side at about the same time. They bobbed in and out of the saucepan, sitting up to rotate an oatmeal flake in slender fingers as they daintily nibbled it. The remote possibility that they might carry illness or parasites harmful to humans never entered our thoughts. We were too enchanted to worry.

We decided to try our luck at fishing before the air warmed up. But after several hours, it became obvious there was no catch. I looked at my husband's discouraged expression and felt like crying. He had wanted so much to get away, to do a little, peaceful fishing and go back to work refreshed and proud of having accomplished something.

The previous winter in the Uintas had been dry as their winters go, not as much snowfall as expected. Unknown to us, this meant that the level of China Lake would be down, the rivers no more than streams, with only fingerling trout to tease at our bait.

Later, upon our return home, we were to mention this absolute paucity of tight lines.

"Yes, we didn't like it up there," said the fishing enthusiast's wife. "The water disappointed us."

How much would it have cost her to have spoken up earlier when her husband was recommending the place? We will never know. Obviously, she did not dare correct his faulty memory in front of him and did not care enough about us to contact me privately later on. Another lesson well-learned, but I resisted the impulse to commit mayhem.

Anyway, as they say, we took down the tent and moved on. After more exploring on back roads, we found State Highway 150, and arriving late, camped that night along the Hayden Fork of the Bear River. Since it's at a slightly lower elevation (9,100'), we awoke a little less chilled the following morning, but still watched the sun steaming frost off the shrubbery along the river.

Yet no one could have prepared us for awakening at this second campsite. I couldn't believe the sounds we were hearing. My stomach tightened into a fistful of knots. Where on earth had we camped? The animal sounds were headed right for us. We were going to be caught in the middle of a stampede!

By now, my husband was wide awake, too. "What the devil is that?" he demanded. Hurriedly, I unzipped a window of the tent to look outside. Sheep! Domestic sheep.

Sheep? We were in a wilderness area. Weren't we? But sheep it was. I clutched my stomach, feeling foolish but glad.

A large flock was being moved through the

meadow on the other side of a split rail fence next to us. The sharp barking of the black-and-white border collie carried clearly in the frozen air.

Then came the herder on horseback. "Whup, whup!" he called, then "Yo-o!"

His calls pierced the morning. A few minutes later, another helper arrived, pushed a bicycle out of sight into the bushes, and then began tossing pebbles at the more rebellious sheep.

The baa-ing had crescendoed but the dong-dong of the bellwether still eclipsed it all. Without realizing it, we had managed to camp on a sheep ranch inside Wasatch National Forest, which borders the Uintas. In fact, the line between the Forest and the wilderness is indistinguishable. And in the twilight, we had not seen the small roadside signs. Even so, what was a sheep ranch doing in a National Forest?

Later, we learned from the U.S. Forest Service that a few grazing permittees do run sheep and some cattle in this way. I'm glad we checked it out because no one else believed our story.

If it meant being frozen, frightened and enchanted all over again, if we could laugh and cry, we would do it again in a minute. Camping in the Uinta Mountains of Utah was an unforgettable experience.

# # #

Old Age? We'd Better Start It Young!

Most of us hope to be liked and respected when we are old. Most of us want to think people will say nice things about us then. Yet will we be pleasant enough to deserve those reactions? Or will we find ourselves among the many elderly who have negative attitudes, even IF they are relatively pain-free and have the necessities of life? Of course, that's a mighty big IF, as many of us already know from our own or friends' personal experience.

It is often easier not to think about what might lie ahead. Yet unless we stop and look at our probable futures, we will arrive at our destination unprepared. To begin that, we must first face the reality that life is not fair. Many people fall victim to the inequalities in the world. These are legion, so I will mention only a few:

sheer bad luck with one calamity following

another;

being female or a minority in a society that despises you;

falling through the gaping holes in our society's flimsy safety nets;

losing health insurance with no government program to fill the gap;

being denied workmen's compensation for job-related illnesses and injuries;

having children who turn out to be dismal failures or even criminals;

being robbed of our life savings by white collar criminals who get away with it.

Outside of those issues, which often can and do hit innocent people at random, it can be our own actions (or their lack) that get us into whatever predicament we land in.

Betrayal, disgust over deteriorating social

mores, political chicanery or other tragic reversals can turn the sunniest Pollyanna into vinegar, and rightfully so. Some cranky dispositions encountered among those reaching senior citizen status can be blamed on a disappointing retirement outlook or on the onset of senility. But not all. Nor can crabbiness be supposed the natural result of greater susceptibility to illness and injuries. (While serious aches and pains are immensely distressing, they are certainly not just a liability of old age.) Quite often, lack of foresight or earlier foolish decisions made (by oneself or a spouse) cause much of the unhappiness in older citizens.

It is unlikely that we can forever cheat the major illnesses that debilitate. Neither can we hold back the normal effects of aging, nor do much more than protest vehemently when the government unfeelingly cuts social programs on which we based a chunk of our financial decisions while in the work force.(Or politicians flat out lie to us, making promises they have no intention of keeping.) But since today we pay for decisions made yesterday, we can also start planning now to be old. The following aspects of our lives can be pondered.

First, persistent refusal to eat anything but junk food over the years, and/or indulgence in cigarettes or alcoholic beverages, destroys mind and body far earlier than nature intended. An individual's family must then bear the physical, emotional and financial burden of around-the-clock care, either at home or in an often low-quality nursing home.

Our small group of relatives suffered acutely under the strain of coping with one individual's stubborn, hostile mother who had driven herself into premature debility and senility by foolish health practices over many years. Unwilling to find out the facts first, lower-echelon hospital officials recently attacked her husband for starving her, an outrageous accusation, since the woman repeatedly refused to eat, no matter what was put in front of her. It was more likely an inevitable stage of the dying process, something the hospital should have recognized.

The husband still loved his wife too much to fix the blame where it belonged and did not defend himself very well to officials. He was forced to have someone with her practically 24 hours a day, under threat of being sent to jail, if he left her alone for more than fifteen minutes. None of this made any difference in her eating habits.

Second, rest and recreation are probably most overlooked by the working-class and middle-class who are approaching middle age. Short of money though many of us are from raising a family and helping out our parents, we must use some of our income to provide escape for ourselves. Such enjoyment is more important than buying name brand clothing for our children, for example. Teenagers should be earning their own clothing money if they cannot exist without someone else's name plastered across their hips!

Third, financial problems bedevil some of the elderly, as they do all age groups. At all stages of life, we need minimal insurance for health, life, fire and auto, but why be over-insured? Too, everyone needs a small savings account for short-term goals, and another for long-term. Admittedly, saving anything is disheartening because (1) any interest earned is frequently taxable and (2) unexpected bills can wipe out our nest egg. Still, if we had not built that fund, we would be worse off.

Related to this subject is the conviction that both men and women should obtain as much formal and informal education as possible. Updated skills are always useful. And if we stop learning about our world, we gullible, greedy younger people easily become gullible, bitter older people. Exercise of the mind is the greatest antidote to losing mental acuity.

Another concern for our elderly (that is, for our future selves) is social difficulties: they may lack transportation or may have been denied a driver's license because of diminished faculties; they may have children too busy or too far away to help them, or children angry over past family disagreements. On the other hand, there may be no children, no nieces or nephews.

We must face the painful fact that not only can we not always rely on our children in the future, but they may even try in various ways to harm us. If they do help us, we can rejoice, but today's society does not feel the same sense of responsibility for parents as did previous generations. We should have a network of friends and associates to whom we can also turn. But building these friendships takes years of genuine caring.

We must develop hobbies at the earliest opportunity, or join associations of people with similar interests, to prevent isolation and loneliness. Learning to use our time alone creatively will bring out hidden talents or strengths. Additionally, if those relatives we expect to visit us, do not do so, the greater loss will be to them.

Church activity fills a void for many but none

of us can expect others of our own faith to fill all of our needs. Besides, if we restrict our good acquaintances to such a narrow group, we will miss many of the rewarding experiences the world has to offer.

Nowadays, a major worry is crime. In those rural areas which have experienced rapid growth, older people still have a rural mentality; they resist both adaptation to the changes brought by increasing urbanization and recognition of stresses and social rules of crowded living.

Our former, small-town neighborhood was terrorized for over a year by teenage intruders while the police seemed incapable of identifying them. Yet I had naive neighbors who refused to install strong locks, still others who thought me paranoid because I locked my doors and windows in the daytime. Apparently, city dwellers are more likely to take steps to try to protect themselves.

During our preparations to meet old age, we must also become self-reliant. A whining adult is no more attractive than a whining child. At the same time, we must recognize that sometimes we will have to accept help graciously, and not be insulted at every imagined slight to our independence.

We must pay attention to where we are living now, its advantages and disadvantages. If we stay, can we get to the store safely? What if the store were torn down? Can we get to the Golden Hours Center to be with other people? Will we want to? Or will we sit home and sulk as my Great Auntie Dolly did?

Great Auntie Dolly sat in her house, waiting to die. She was not poor and her mind was still sharp, yet she refused to read. She got rid of her television and rarely turned on her ancient radio. She could not be bothered to write letters or send cards, even when her niece and nephew provided stationery and stamps. She refused to wear her hearing aid when relatives visited, and complained loudly every time because they did not stay longer or visit more often.

Dreams die. Noblest ambitions falter. Tragedy spears us. Betrayal destroys our faith in humanity and in God. Disillusionment sets in early in life sometimes. That does not give us the right, at any age, to vent our rage and frustration on those who are not responsible for our suffering.

If we dare not express our anger at those who *are* at fault, then instead we can keep working for our civil rights or those of others, we can chop logs, or we can throw old china at the back fence with great enthusiasm. But also, we must salvage what we can of our crumbled castle walls and achieve whatever goals we may. If we have none left, we must set aside our cynicism and establish new ones, even if sorrow limits today's goal to "I will smile at one friendly and one grouchy person that I meet."

Perhaps we will die tomorrow and not have to worry about old age. But we cannot count on that! I, for one, hope not to be one of the unhappy old people I encounter so often in my life, unhappy because they did not plan to be old. That said, the best laid plans of mice and women often go astray.

# # #

It Isn't Too Late to Make a Change

Easier said than done?

How many of us haven't had to give up hobbies, cancel vacation plans, or postpone pursuit of goals because of job or family responsibilities, an accident, or a financial setback? Even more often, though, the frustration is likely to be the result of letting everyday chores, unnecessary "busy work," or the opinion of others get in our way, or of letting unnoticed expenses drain our bank accounts.

Standing in the check-out line at the drug store, Jolene, a harried young mother, was riffling the pages of a crafts magazine when the grey-haired woman behind her spoke up. "You look so wistful, honey."

Jolene quickly rescued the magazine from the grasp of her two-year-old, who let out a howl.

"Oh, it's all this neat stuff!--*Mandy, hush now--*

I don't have time for projects nowadays," she said.

"You can make the time."

Jolene groaned. "Don't I wish! Working full-time! And with my husband and the baby!"

But the woman cheerfully insisted. "You can do it. You can give up something else."

Jolene shook her head. "There's dinner, and dishes, and laundry and cleaning."

The older woman paused, then said, "Well, I know better than to tell you to ask your husband to help out. So many of them won't."

"You can say that again! And it isn't because he doesn't know how!" Jolene started to unload her purchases on to the counter.

"Could you squeak by if you only worked part-time?"

"Oh, *I* think so, but he likes the extra money."

"Now that's a problem!" She was silent for a

moment. "We were tied to our jobs for years. Then my husband got sick--"

"And now you can't go anywhere?" guessed Jolene.

"Right. Or do anything much. Even if he weren't sick, inflation—we waited too long, that's all."

Later, Jolene's thoughts returned to that unexpected conversation. She couldn't convince her husband to help with the chores or to let her work only part-time, but now, while he lies in front of the television after dinner, she relaxes, too. As soon as Mandy is in bed, Jolene does macramé or bead work, or studies books on ceramics and weaving. She had given up those interests when she got married because her husband thought they were a waste of time and money. She also has an answer ready in the event he starts complaining about the untidy apartment.

Not reaching desired goals because we feel the need to take life easy for a while is one thing.

Not following ambitions because something or someone else blocks our path is quite another. An ant is not often forced to be a grasshopper, after all. But in today's world, he or she is frequently coerced into being the wrong species of ant.

Could it be time for us to set aside those "needs" that have cluttered center stage long enough in our lives? Sometimes we can stubbornly say, "Enough! No more wasteful meetings with other people this summer," or "We're not subscribing to any more magazines that we aren't going to read!" In other cases, like Jolene, we may need to be prodded into making changes, into overcoming roadblocks.

Women without children often have problems equally as frustrating as Jolene's. Nancy, a career woman in her thirties, had often been stymied over flying from Los Angeles to New York to see her family: The timing of available vacation slots conflicted with night school classes related to her job. Her services were also in demand as a church volunteer; and a married sister nearby often relied on her as a last-minute babysitter.

Finally, in annoyed desperation, Nancy looked at the upcoming two-week break in her schooling, told her boss an emergency had come up back home, and made airline reservations before anyone could find something else for her to do. The visit included two days with her grandmother. A couple of months later, when her grandma died, Nancy felt good because she had done what she wanted to do.

This is not to say we should feel guilty if we failed to accomplish such a trip "in time." Each situation is unique and impossibility sometimes wins out. If Nancy had not found a way to pay for the tickets, she would not have been able to take the trip, no matter how much she wanted it. Nothing is more destructive than accepting unwarranted guilt placed on us by others.

Sometimes it is a lack of money, as much as lack of time, that makes people hesitate to do what they really want to do. We suffer through years of frustration at not being able to purchase an item that, while not falling into the realm of fantasy, still will not fit in our budget. David and Susan, owners of a fine new stereo system, recently commented, "We always said if we wait till we can actually afford to buy it, we'll never get it."

Perhaps feeling that some of us who heard the comment were silently accusing them of being foolish, David added, "Hey, don't get us wrong! If we eat out nowadays, it's at McDonald's, not The Fireside Inn, but it's worth it."

Added Susan, "To us, beautiful music just isn't beautiful on cheap, tacky equipment."

Maybe the decision we need to make involves an activity largely unrelated to our present lifestyle or one that would alter the way we live. In this case, fear of what others may say or of what the future may hold is often the obstruction. Keeping in mind our responsibility to our family, does it really matter if we do not become the most valuable employee, or the boss? What do we have invested in the pension plan that goes with the hated job?

Is it really important to be accepted into a possibly cliquey fraternal organization or auxiliary? Few people will care while we are alive, and even less will remember after we are dead. It is natural to want to feel important and worthwhile but our other yearnings could bring us the same or greater satisfaction.

What else could we be doing with our time? While none of us has the right to abandon those dependent on us for food, clothing and shelter, any additional, selfish demands on their part can choke off our development. Conversely, too many outside pressures can disrupt the normal closeness of a family, if not squelched at the source. Finding the right balance is a lifelong juggling skill.

If we are secretly unhappy, or openly so, we should start making plans for at least improving our situation, if the actual change is beyond us at this time. We can write letters to obtain information. We can open the savings account. We can track down the high school friend with whom we once shared dreams, till marriage pulled us apart. The time and money for undertakings like these can be found, even if it's in installments.

With any luck, our homes and yards will not become the eyesores of the neighborhood as we pursue revived interests or new freedoms, but they will survive a few extra days without maintenance or new plantings. Dirt damages paint and fabric, but we can leave a car unwashed just this once, the carpet un-vacuumed today. Spoiled Mama or mother-in-law can wait a couple more days for her thrice-monthly letter, even if it precipitates a scolding long-distance phone call from her the first few times the letter is a day and a half late.

The nineteenth century poet John Greenleaf

Whittier wrote in 1856 in *Maud Muller*:

> *For of all sad words of tongue or pen,*
>
> *The saddest are these: "It might have*
>
> *been!"*

Too often we find ourselves, or think ourselves, hemmed in by past decisions. We convince ourselves or allow others to convince us that we now cannot do those things we always wanted to try. There is no time; there is no money.

As one who completed my bachelor's degree at the age of 41, I know that the "path not taken" is often only on the other side of trees and bushes. We can find a narrow footpath, even a rabbit tunnel through the shrubs, that will let us fight our way across, and at least take a look at that other version of a possibly more meaningful life. We may find that we want nothing to do with vaunted higher education and its academic backstabbing, or the golf circuit or cruises to Mexico, or that we never use the DVD player we finally bought. Or we may find new joy and meaning in life. Either way, afterward, "if only" will no longer haunt us.

Getting a project launched or obtaining some free time for ourselves will lessen our feelings of helplessness and frustration, while diminishing our depression and disillusionment. In the long run, <u>everyone</u> benefits when someone else is no longer seething with rage and frustration. Taking long-thwarted steps toward our own personal goals will make us more amiable and interesting, as well as give us a more charitable outlook toward life in general.

# # #

Defeating the Tyranny of the Telephone

Let's face it. The telephone is the bane and the miracle of our private life in today's world, especially since we got cell phones and now so-called smartphones, which are actually dumber than dumb. But that's another story! And with cellphones, it is the owners who need to be reminded even more about good manners, not to mention safe usage.

Blessings first: It's reassuring to know I can call for emergency help, assuming I can reach a telephone, and assuming that the 911 number is not tied up with stupid calls from people wanting directions to the nearest pizza parlor. (If you don't believe me, attend a few neighborhood watch meetings with your local police department.) In pre-telephone days, it was much more difficult to summon help -- from anyone.

Also, it saves time, money and disappointment to call ahead to find out if a store has an item in stock, to order tickets, or to make appointments or reservations, and so forth.

Finally, for most people, the greatest blessing of the telephone is its ability to put us in touch with a friendly voice after a harrowing experience, or during an extended separation. With the increased and not-altogether-welcome mobility of this generation, our best friend or favorite sibling may be clear across town or thousands of miles away.

Letters are often the best form of communication, since they can be read over and over to ease loneliness and grief, or to share happiness. But the majority of people either have little inclination to write, or face such heavy report writing on the job that the sight of another notepad or keyboard at home makes them ill. In these situations, the telephone provides an immediate boost to morale when we need it.

On the down side, it has been considered good manners to answer the telephone before its second or third ring. I have always found this particular rule of etiquette to be impractical. It is also presumptuous of the caller even to expect me to gallop through the house immediately, trying to find the phone to answer such an imperious summons. Five or six rings is more practical, even though we can then expect the caller to demand "Where were you?!" as though it were any of their business that I was wiping cobwebs off the chandelier on the maid's day off.

On the other hand, too often the caller lets the phone ring eight or ten or 17 times, perhaps waking us out of a deep sleep, and then it turns out to be a wrong number or worse, a whiskey-throated old biddy trying to sell us magazine subscriptions. Did you know answering machines and voice mail don't give a lot of choices on how many rings you can select before they pick up?

We are foolish to upset or injure ourselves rushing to answer a ringing phone. Those who know us should be told that it may ring up to six times before we pick it up. And for people who don't know us? "If it's important, they'll call back."

Frankly, people seem not to realize that the person being called is the one who determines just how fast, or even if, the phone is answered. Those calling often give no thought as to time of day or whether the callee might be trying to eat a decent meal, rest a sore back on a heating pad, or soak in the tub after an unnerving battle with crosstown traffic.

Having an unlisted telephone number would cut down considerably on unwanted calls, were it not that every merchant in town insists on having your phone number on checks and charge slips. It's been my experience that if you refuse to provide that information, they will not sell you what you came in to buy, unless you then proffer cash.

Obnoxious salespersons or pesky survey-takers never do call at convenient times, but neither do some long-winded relatives or acquaintances. Many individuals become enraged at encountering an answering machine on a residence telephone line, but such an invention screens out a lot of time-wasters whose calls do not deserve to be acknowledged. (Try telling that to your forgetful 80-year-old mother, however, when she's in nagging mode at 2 a.m.)

Those people who refuse to leave messages on answering machines have only themselves to blame when they cannot reach an individual. Of course, individuals who hide behind their machines, never returning its messages, eventually find themselves in serious trouble and/or friendless.

We had an answering machine (a gift) but it persistently refused to shut off after a message had been left, using up an hour's worth of tape on one short call. Its so-called free warranty service required a stiff "handling charge" which we were not willing to pay. So we only turned on the machine when expecting a very important call. Even then, a less crucial call sometimes got in first, using up all the tape. We hope to buy a better brand soon.

Alexander Graham Bell knew that his invention would change forever the way people lived. Although he expected a few disadvantages to the telephone, he would be aghast at the flagrant abuse that has accompanied its use over the past 30 years.

If, while attempting to gain control over the telephone in our home, we find that we can also afford the cost of a mechanical secretary to make life less hectic, so much the better. Anything that defeats the tyranny of the telephone should be welcomed into our lives.

# # #

The Butterfly

I wanted to make a memory box to hang on the living-room wall. For this I needed: seeds, a quaint old bottle, a miniature carved animal, a pine cone, perhaps some dried flowers, a treasured photograph and, I thought, a butterfly. We were experiencing a migration of beautiful and harmless Painted Ladies. To see them fluttering over a field bright with dandelions was a glorious sight

I told my husband about the memory box and that I needed a butterfly. I asked him to keep for me any dead one he might come across. But it is hard to find a dead butterfly that has not been mutilated, often from colliding with a car or other solid object. My husband finally concluded that I would have to catch a live one and kill it, but I balked at that idea.

Then one afternoon, I came across a dying butterfly. I knew he was feeble for he fluttered only a few inches away when I reached for him.

On the third try, I caught him gently and carried him into the house.

Yet as I watched him struggle, I pondered upon that fragile life, that spark of intelligence the small creature possessed. His life and migration had already been a beauty and a marvel. In his brief span of time, he had accomplished the work he had been on earth to do. And that was so much more memorable than any post-mortem exhibition could be.

# # #

The Express Checkout

It seems that courtesy and a few genuine smiles may have become as extinct as the dinosaurs for the city dwellers of the 2010s. Far too frequently, we shove each other out of the way in pursuit of the necessities of day-to-day living.

Of course, rudeness exists everywhere, not just in cities. Each of us is born rather ill-mannered; innocent babies are very demanding people. But in most cultures, given merely an average childhood, we learn that others have rights, too, rights that must be considered; we learn the rules of society.

Yet the cultural shock of returning to a metropolitan area following a 12-year stay in a rural state can be substantial. We urbanites seem to care little nowadays that those around us are also human beings, with despairs and joys, heartaches and triumphs, often suffering from loneliness, sometimes giddy with good fortune. One reason for the indifference is the overcrowding, which brings out unkind instincts in humans, just as it does in other life forms. For example, just stopping at the store in the city to buy a gallon of milk is a very different experience than doing so in a smaller town.

Standing in a supermarket express line in my new location, I soon realize we are going to move at less than breakneck speed. In front of the young executive carrying raw mushrooms and a bottle of Chablis, and an elderly gentleman with a pint of milk, a woman unloads a pile of groceries that exceeds the ten-item limit. I groan inwardly while others gripe aloud. She chooses not to hear us.

After ringing up 17 items, the harried checker snaps at the older matron. "It's $27.46 but next time, don't stand in this line when you have that many items!"

I flinch at the tone of voice, feeling instant sympathy for its victim. While I more than empathize with the frustration and annoyance, the checker's attitude jars. She lacks the manners to say "shouldn't." Instead, it is plain "don't," as though she were dealing with an obstreperous child. This is another adult she is addressing, one older than she and one who has not said or done anything nasty, after all.

But who knows? This may well be the eleventh time in just one shift that it has happened to that checker. And too many people do brazen their way through life at the expense of the rest of us, frequently responding with obscenities if challenged.

When the customer says nothing, the fuzzy-faced bagger chimes in. "You can't stand in the express line when you have so many things. Everyone knows that." His is the arrogance of youth.

The woman still does not answer, does not blush, and simply begins to rummage in her purse for money. Perhaps a minute goes by, two. She seems immune to being scolded by strangers in front of strangers, and by individuals young enough to be her child and grandchild at that.

"$27.46," repeats the cashier. "Can't you hurry? Look at the line!"

The woman's ears and neck flush bright red. Her mouth twitches as if she is about to cry. The resentment of other customers now turns to embarrassment. We look at the floor, out the window, anywhere but at the culprit. It is an exasperating and possibly deliberate violation of the store's rules, one for which the woman should have been taken to task. Yet the reprimand has become unjust humiliation.

Then comes a twinge at my conscience. I could speak up, say something like, "Look, miss, she made me furious, too, but enough's enough. Leave the woman alone!"

On the other hand, perhaps it is better that none of us says much. I'm not sure anyone has enough facts to interfere. It is possible that by playing dumb, this same woman gets away with her rule-flouting behavior in every store she enters.

After ransacking her purse, the woman finds enough coins to finish paying her bill, while the grumbling behind her increases. By this time, I feel disgusted with people in general. Civilization often seems not to have done that much for human nature. The veneer over "me first" is very thin: Some people get their own way because of their size. Others use the disposition of a sabre-toothed tiger to challenge their city jungle environment; Others just play stupid.

Afterward, while the checker rings up the purchases of the young executive, the old gentleman between us insists that I set down my gallon of milk. My chilled hands are happy to comply.

The paunchy man in the electric blue jogging suit behind me continues to cradle his Smirnoff and his cornflakes, not setting them on the moving belt. My helper puts another divider in place, and then tries in vain to persuade the "jogger" to set down his purchases; the man's mind is elsewhere. Thoroughly miffed, the senior citizen returns the second divider to its rack, muttering as he does so. He has probably spent his entire life offering help whether or not it is needed, but it is refreshing to find someone who is trying to be courteous.

After paying his bill, the senior citizen approaches the automatic doors and is almost bowled over by an athletic type striding in, arms swinging. Alarmed, the old man throws out his left arm, as though holding a shield.

"Watch it," he warns. "Watch it now!" He sounds frightened, evidence of a painful memory surfacing.

A few minutes later, he gets into his Buick and starts the engine. As I walk by, I see him adjust his brown fedora, see his mouth settle into a tight line. Now that he is behind the wheel, his personality changes. Sadly, it has to, or he will not survive in frenetic traffic. Yet, hopefully, the man has not metamorphosed into today's arrogant, devil-take-you maniac of city driving.

At one time, being "from the city" meant one had a certain degree of polish, of urbanity. Has that city life faded into a shadow of its former self? Or did it never really exist? Perhaps 12 years in a rural state distorted my memories of living in a metropolis.

# # #

Someday My Ship Will Come In

Ever wondered who came up with the notion of *Someday my ship will come in?* If we've just accepted it as part of our western culture, then not a few of us have only half-jokingly added, "When my ship comes in, I'll probably be at the airport."

The truth of the expression is likely to be much older than we realize. British merchants in the 19th century built and sent out many of those Tall Ships. Now we love to watch them, whenever the rebuilt originals and/or replicas sail up the coasts and into harbors across the United States and Canada. There is nothing in this world like the sight of sail, on the open sea or coming into safe harbor. Outside of early explorers who sailed "for the Crown," those British merchants, along with the Dutch, French, Germans, Portuguese, Spanish, and others, invested almost everything they owned, hoping it would pay off in the return of a great fortune for them.

Long before the Europeans, as we know them

today, Minoan and Phoenician traders outfitted merchant ships and sent them on long voyages, never knowing when they'd return, filled with incredible discoveries and fat profits for the merchants. The Phoenicians may even have navigated as far as modern day Brazil.

Often years slipped by, as a ship explored, with no messages received back home. Sometimes the ship and its crew perished. Even the Vikings were forced to trade with communities too strong to be plundered, yet perhaps half of them died at sea on one of countless voyages of discovery, rape and pillage. Few shed tears on their behalf, however. Though family ties were less important in some cultures than in others, the loneliness and heartache for families left behind seems unbearable to us, from our vantage point of instant communication. Yet that is the only life they knew.

Perhaps you can see where I'm going with this. We need to invest in ourselves as writers and in our product(s). If one ship (book) founders, we know we'll be OK, if we're working on the second or the third book. Our articles and essays may drown in a sea of submissions, rejected by twenty-something editors, who know little about our field of expertise, or life as it is actually lived. Never mind. We can self-publish, or we can write for the Internet. But what we write must be good, must be nearly perfect in every way. I might get away with spelling errors or using the wrong word in informal writing, but I can't do that in my books, or anywhere else I expect to be taken seriously.

With recognition, even fame, comes responsibility to your readers. This is no arena for the haughty. And as you send out your ships, please remember to protect the privacy of your lifestyle and the safety of your family.

So, what kind of ships can we send out in the reality of today's overpriced everything? We can't invest all of our assets in unproven ventures, even if they have worked well for other writers. And what if we do send out ships and hear nothing back? Just remember those long voyages of earlier days, and consider the future long treks in space exploration. The payoff is there; it is only delayed.

Here are a few suggestions for ships you may want to send out:

Tell people you're a writer, but first practice what you'll say next.

Don't be a snob, but choose your associates wisely. There's little use telling a person about your inspirational romance novel, when she's wallowing in profanity herself.

Send out postcards of your book cover, but if you can't afford them, always have business cards with you wherever you go. Try vistaprint.com for free cards that have minimal advertising on the back.

Brochures? Yes, if they look professional. Better to carry a crisp black-and-white tri-fold from a laser printer than a blurry color job from anything else.

Keep your resume current and focused for a

particular type of writing assignment. That means having several versions of it, in hard copy and electronic formats.

Look for online forums where you *can add value to a discussion*. Resist the urge to just jump in, say something trite, and spam everyone with a five-line signature.

IF you carry out any or all of the above positive suggestions, there'll be more possibilities for billowing sails above a heavy cargo outside the lagoon, rather than tattered sails limping around the breakwater. That said, many a weary sailing vessel finally made it home victorious. And if the hold is only half-filled with treasures, that is success, too. Doing something about your dream is what makes the difference. Doing nothing means your life will not change.

# # #

Doing It Right No Longer Seems to Matter

It can't just be bad luck, but neither can my husband and I have angered anyone enough to justify our being singled out for such generally incompetent service as we've been receiving in recent years. While we generally try to maintain a positive attitude toward the twists and turns of life, this poor service is happening, so much so that it must also be going on all around us, driving other people crazy, too.

Regardless of who we deal with--tradesperson, sales office, insurance claims adjustor, dispensing optician's lab, car repair shop, bank card processing center--the odds are short that somewhere along the line, the process will go awry. Doing it right no longer seems to matter.

A number of people are wonderfully courteous while they make their inexplicable mistakes--"sweet idiots" my husband calls them. Yet a little cynicism is nudging its way into our attitudes now. Incompetence is so commonplace that we no longer really expect anything to be done right the first time. Of course, we then enjoy that delightful surprise when something does go right. For example, when we added an item of value to the personal articles floater attached to our homeowners insurance, it was handled both promptly and correctly. Thanks, Vic. We appreciated that.

Certainly not just uncaring sales clerks or poorly-trained tellers spoil the reputations of their conscientious colleagues and provide their customers with inconveniences and delays that could easily have been avoided. Often, a situation is out of the control of the local representative.

For instance, we recently ordered electronics equipment for a family member to use in his employment. It did not arrive at the retail store when it was supposed to, nor did it come the following week. After the equally angry, frustrated store manager made a phone call to the opposite coast, the test equipment was sent out. But it is minus a critical part of the order, so still cannot be used.

A popular but expensive photographic filter, paid for in advance -- as required at another establishment -- and promised for delivery in ten days, did not arrive for 3-1/2 months, with no explanations being given for the delay, in spite of numerous inquiries. The outing that had required the use of the filter came and went, as did several others.

Likewise, our bank promptly processed my check guarantee card application but lost my husband's. He filled out another form for me to take back to the bank's apologetic employee and will continue to wait in hope. His alternative is to keep living without what many merchants insist on seeing before they accept a check. And "experts" wonder why so many people charge their purchases.

Turning to things medical: Six weeks ago, I ordered bifocal eyeglasses with a light tint (Grey #1) to cut glare from indoor lighting. The lab manufactured the lenses as trifocals. The order was resubmitted. The lab then manufactured the glasses as bifocals with Grey #6 coloring, a much darker shade. I am still waiting for the prescription to be filled correctly.

Trying to get numerous legitimate medical claims paid has been an exercise in massive futility and frustration over a ten-month period. With one exception, every claim submitted to the health insurance company was processed incorrectly or not at all. Only notification of serious intent to file a lawsuit finally got corrective action from a senior official in the company. However, we are still waiting for the largest reimbursement to be sent to us.

It isn't just the insurance side of it that has been alarming. Once, a highly-delicate medical procedure was almost performed on me without my being given allergy-suppressant medication during the preceding 24 hours. A previous test had revealed my allergic reaction to the proposed contrast agent and there was a note to that effect in my file. Only my reminding the attending nurse of my allergy at the last moment prevented a possible disaster.

I fully realize that medical personnel are overworked but at least one someone in a position of responsibility should have checked my file the day before. No one did.

Two major surgeries, though competently performed, have left me with unpleasant side effects, the likelihood of which was not explained in advance. My medical history indicates that I face at least one more possible surgery, for a condition unrelated to the others, at some time in the future. I should recuperate beautifully, according to the latest physicians. They've got to be kidding. With everything else that's been happening, I'm cheerfully going to put myself in harm's way again?   I would first like to feel confident that doing it right does indeed matter.

# # #

Of Tents and Thistles and Things

Tenting is for the stalwart – those who will remain unwavering in the face of bugs, bumps and things that get lumpy in the night. It isn't for anyone whose thinly clad legs and ankles object to thistles.

When my grade school art classes were asked to show our summer vacation, I drew a tent surrounded by thistles, in angry Technicolor. At the age of six, I'd been taken by my parents to Pagham, near Bognor Regis, England. It was the first vacation I'd experienced, although not the first I'd want to remember. My sister was close on three years old then and prone to being high-strung. This was a polite way of saying she threw tantrums when she didn't want to do something. She was also cutting molars at the time. Poor mother!

On arrival, we had got down from the train at the long end of the platform. Of course, the engineer had to stop where it was convenient for the train, not for us, hence the name, the long end of the platform. After walking "about a mile" back to the station house, we were able to hail a taxicab, a major luxury on our minuscule budget.

Our destination was a huge, empty field. Huge, that is, to a child's eyes. Empty, that is, of everything but funny brown things flapping in the wind and giant weeds-with-thorns. The cab driver wasn't surprised; he said he came this way often in the summer.

I don't remember where or what we ate. How we slept, or what shared our bedding with us, remains a mystery. The kind of bathroom privileges we did or didn't have must not have been important, probably an enamel chamber pot of some kind.

I do remember brushing my teeth in a tin mug of water, and wading through thistles, bawling at the top of my lungs. Feverish little sister was carried to and from the tent. I know we stayed at least three days before getting back on the train. Mother was all but gibbering by the time we got home that year.

There were no more vacations till I was 9 or 10 years old. That summer we rented the family doctor's caravan at Swanage, England. This was camping in style! The caravan was parked on a farm along with others, about half-a-mile from the beach. Vividly do I remember that farm. I fell into the stream retrieving a tennis ball that the farmer's daughter had overthrown. In the process, I ruined the only pair of sandals I owned.

The farm's gander, hissing and flapping, chased any guest who ventured near the farmyard. He was an unbeatable and rather terrifying "watchdog." Charlie, their big, bay horse bit two children while we were there, even though we'd all been warned of his short temper.

Some two years later, we rented another caravan at Milford-on-Sea, also in England. A nearby pond produced swarms of midges. But we also got the best fish and chips we'd ever tasted!

They were cooked over a coal fire in a large white van that came to the camp.

I was past my teens and in the United States before I had contact with any more camping vacations. This was a group adventure, families and singles. It was pretty exciting to be invaded by shiny, young faces while taking a nap. But the wanderings soon became so accepted that no more violent reaction than a sleepy "Oh, hi! Looking for mommy's tent?" was ever heard. Today we would not dare let our child wander!

Another camping experience comes to mind, that being a tent trailer in the high desert. This one involved two adult couples and one couple's two children. That fact alone made it an interesting way to test an old friendship. Weather-wise, it turned cold enough at night that the heater had to be used. A high wind came up and, by next morning, sand had invaded everything. Hay fever set in with a vengeance for one wife.

And then there was the state park area near Pt. Mugu, California. (And surely, at similar coastal locations around this nation.) At any age, that's what camping's all about! Exhilarating mornings with the Pacific Ocean's air in your lungs, bacon crisping in the pan outside the tent, a shy chipmunk growing bolder...relaxation...pure happiness.

The only thing to beat that is parking your car at a trailhead, backpacking and pitching your tent in some barely touched glen, with a fresh trout over the embers. And serenity, solitude and serendipity all around you. Or as I have previously written, camping in the Uintas is an experience unique to itself.

# # #

Mom, My Shoes Are Still in the River

Now that the picnic season is upon us, I am reminded of an experience my husband and I had with our youngsters.

One Saturday afternoon, I was staring into the open refrigerator when the seven-year-old twins, Reg and Ron, thundered across the kitchen floor. "What's to eat, Mom?"

"I guess it's hamburgers," I said.

"All RIGHT! Let's go on a picnic, Mom!" they said.

Four-year-old Jennifer chimed in. "Please, Mommy, please!"

"Well, if Daddy . . . ."

"Yay!" yelled the twins. They raced out into the yard.

"Daddy, we're going on a picnic!" Ron announced. "Can you get the charcoal an' stuff?"

I wasn't too worried about my husband's response, since he doesn't mind cooking on the portable grill. But when Reg invited two of our new neighbors to go with us, I scrabbled through the kitchen catch-all drawer for the slip of paper that held their parents' phone number. Why it wasn't on the refrigerator door, I don't know.

Mrs. Chandler reassured me. "Oh, Erik and Gretchen will love that! Mind if we come along?"

We were ready to leave in less than thirty minutes, and didn't forget a thing.

Our two-car caravan had barely arrived at a nearby park when all five children made a frantic dash for the swings and slides section. The clutter of toys and baseball gear they had insisted on bringing was abandoned, something I had expected to happen.

The guys carefully checked the direction of the prevailing breeze before lighting the charcoal. It didn't make any difference. We still waved and coughed at each other through a blue haze until the briquettes had banked. Then the wind miraculously vanished. We started cooking and spread out the other food.

Suddenly, a faint cry for help reached us, accompanied by much giggling. Then we saw a big guy from a nearby family group carrying a wet, muddy Reg toward us.

"Reginald Andrew!" I yelled.

He made a face. "Sorry, Mom! I couldn't help it."

"Thanks," said my husband as Reg's benefactor unloaded him. "I'm sorry we had to bother you."

"No problem," the man said. "Happens to most of us, sooner or later." He shook his head in amusement as he strode back to his own family.

I knew what had happened. Reg wants to be a fighter pilot if he grows up. Privately, his dad and I think he'll be a dowser. His nose leads him to water no matter where we are.

My husband scolded Reg and grounded him. Then he and Mr. C. went to investigate the river. I looked at Reg in dismay. He wasn't wearing his good clothes, of course, but what he had on would have to be hit with the garden hose before being put into the washing machine.

The men returned to report that the river was two feet wide, four inches deep and not a ripple broke the surface. That accounted for the stagnant smell and the mud.

The hot dogs joined the hamburgers on the grill. As I tried to concentrate on keeping them from curling up, Ron squelched up next to me. The same stench that adorned Reg hit me in the face.

I groaned with frustration. "Ron, you've only had those shoes three weeks!"

"Mom," said Reg, "my shoes are still in the river."

Erik volunteered to rescue them.

"No, Erik . . . ," began his mother. But he was gone.

We did manage to bring Jennifer and Gretchen down with clumsy tackles.

"Why don't you big girls watch the table?" I suggested.

"Yes," said Mrs. C., catching her cue. "We don't want the starlings to fly off with the buns."

Jennifer and Gretchen were noisily enthusiastic about this new responsibility.

Mr. C. threw something into the trash can. I peered over his shoulder in time to see it was a badly charred hamburger.

"So you brought hot dogs?! Looks like you were right."

In spite of our efforts, the frankfurters began to form crescent shapes as they cooked. One of them made a bid for freedom and fell into a patch of grass under a tree.

Mrs. C. grabbed for the wiener and threw it back, announcing, "A little grass never hurt anyone!"

"Yeuck," I said, promptly letting another hamburger slide into the coals.

A second later, we both let out a shriek. "It hopped! That wasn't a hot dog! What did you...?"

From our husbands' point of view, it must have been funny. Why else would they have doubled over, shaking?

At this point, Erik returned, backed with mud himself but triumphantly waving Reg's slimy shoes. His father roared, but not with laughter.

Someone discovered we had no can opener.

"Sure we do!" insisted my husband, bringing out his Swiss Army knife.

We set the first can of beans on the grill while we poured fruit juice over the insects that had settled in the paper cups.

"Are you trying to drown the bugs?" a disguised voice asked.

No one had remembered the potholders, so we used tongs to lift the can from the grill, spilling sauce into the hot coals.

"Something's burning, Mommy!" warned Jennifer.

"Well, darn it!" I exclaimed, but actually, it masked the smell radiating from the boys.

Between lots of giggles, everyone stuffed themselves. Finally, clutching her little, round stomach, Jennifer said, "Mommy, this was so much fun!"

Shyly, Gretchen agreed with her. Not to be outdone, all three boys proclaimed the picnic the best time they'd had since they met. Four rather frustrated adults looked at each other, saying nothing. Children can find enjoyment in the most irritating situations.

It was time to pour water over the coals. Steam still rose as we carried the grill back to the curb and set it on the ground to finish cooling. To the best of our knowledge, not more than three near-accidents occurred as passing drivers wondered what was on fire. A couple of cross-country runners barely slowed down to look as they loped by. But the overage hippie we'd seen roaming around sat down on the sidewalk a short distance away to contemplate the steam.

The children were rather quiet on the way home, occupied with something in the back seat. As we neared our street, Jennifer piped, "Mommy, can we go to that park next weekend? Please?"

"We'll have to see," I demurred. "But why next week?"

"Because," said Reg. "These aren't my shoes!"

"Reg!"

"No, Mommy," said Jennifer. "It's 'cause the frog in his pocket will get homesick by then. An' Reg has to put it back under the picnic table ... where he found it."

# # #

When the Whole World Wants You Awake

I moved the drapes another inch, craning my neck.

"So what did they bring home today?" asked my husband from the couch.

I watched in trepidation. Our neighbors dropped the tailgate of their pick-up truck and the red minibike was in full view. But I stalled, anyway. "I can't quite see yet."

They'd moved in six months ago with two boys, three girls and a talking parrot. In succession their family has been joined by two more boys, two collies and a power mower. And the husband has dusted off his trombone.

"Now can you see?" asked my husband.

It rushed out. "A red minibike!"

There was silence for a moment. "It hurts too much to laugh," my husband said. "And I'm too big to cry."

"Not again," I thought. "Not more noise."

In some cultures, an infernal racket during the day is considered normal and few people object to it. If they have to sleep through it, they seem able to, having been conditioned from birth to sleep amid a cacophony of sounds.

In other neighborhoods, a high level of daytime noise around a home is not expected. Anyone from such a background, who has to work nights and is then confronted with multiple oppositions when he tries to sleep during the day, has a terrible time of it. Short of building a home miles from other habitation or an underground shelter in town, it is hard to find a workable solution.

Carla's problems, for example, did not begin until afternoon when her new neighbors' young teenagers got home from school. It was days before Carla got up enough courage to phone a plea to cut the volume of the hard rock music. But she met with instant cooperation. They are good kids. Still, they do have short memories.

Next day the pounding beat was as loud as ever. Half-fearing sarcasm or future harassment, Carla invited them over to hear how it sounded through the wall. They were amazed and apologetic. With a little help from the parents, the stereo was soon moved to an outside wall of the apartment and Carla is happy.

She realizes, however, that not everyone is considerate of other people. "I was really lucky," she admits.

A victim of just that lack of consideration was Hugo, who was almost asleep in his darkened bedroom when the entire apartment building started to vibrate. A now wide-awake Hugo soon identified another tenant's souped-up Chevy being started at full throttle. The noise diminished, crescendoed and was repeated twice. The owner ran back upstairs, leaving the car engine running wide open for a full ten minutes. When the jerk did dash back down to jump in the car, the gasoline fumes had saturated Hugo's bedroom, even with all the windows closed.

The Chevy then screeched out of the driveway, laying down another pall of reeking exhaust. Hugo soon found this was a daily ritual for his neighbor, regardless of the weather or temperature. He put up with the aggravation for several weeks, but then began plotting his revenge.

Non-violent Hugo bought several packages of long tacks to sprinkle in the neighbor's parking slot while he was at work. Halfway to do the job, though, he changed his mind. "I can't do it!" he decided. "If anyone sees me and tells him, I'll be worse off than ever. That won't solve anything."

Complaining to a wishy-washy manager did no good at all. The man himself was too afraid of the roughneck to reprimand him, and the owner lived out-of-state. Hugo has started looking at classified ads, even though he cannot afford to move yet. Moving is his only hope, however, unless the other guy moves first.

The neighborhood tom cat (or for that matter, Thomasina) can be a difficult problem. He often does not restrict his prowling and yowling to just night time. And his owner can hardly be expected to know who is being serenaded each morning (and may not care). Thomas does seem to run out of steam around brunch time, so all you can do is yank another blanket over your head and put cotton balls in your ears till then. Ditto for lonely, tied-up dogs that bark, whine or howl all day.

A far bigger problem, usually, is doorbells, especially if you live alone. You can disconnect the nuisance, if you own your home. If you don't, a landlord may or may not object. Putting neatly-lettered "Day-sleeper," "Do not disturb" or "Do not ring from 8 a.m. to 5 p.m." signs generally does not do any good.

Even in non-wealthy neighborhoods, a stream of solicitors frequently pushes doorbells under such signs, apparently out of sheer perversity. Perhaps, as overgrown children, they want to see if the bell works. Solicitors for anything are not all that welcome at any time, and a day-sleeper awakened by them is likely to give an irate refusal indeed.

For the day-sleeper who has young children at home, life can be a trial for everyone. As Fran, a state trooper's wife said, "Life was much harder when the children were babies. It's impossible for a toddler to understand that he has to be quiet."

Now that the children and their friends are involved in school activities most of the day, Fran's biggest problem is the stream of solicitors. In warm weather, her husband keeps a fan going in the bedroom. This helps to drown out nearby noises.

As most night workers have always known, the biggest bane of their lives until recently has been the telephone. Now, thanks to plug-in jacks, any landline can be silenced whenever the owner wants it that way. Of course, the need to reconnect the phone can be annoying, if not more serious, when for-gotten. Even hearing an answering machine recording while you're trying to sleep isn't always comforting. Maybe we're all going to have cellphones that can be powered off instead, and landlines will go the way of the dodo bird.

An unlisted phone number cuts back considerably on unwanted phone calls, especially those from cranks or sales people. The increase in your monthly phone bill is slight for the convenience you receive. Be sure to give it to important people, such as your employer, best friend and selected relatives.

If you are really on a tight budget, at least try for the cooperation of people you know so that they do not call the house while someone is sleeping, unless it's an emergency.

Perhaps coping with an aspiring opera singer or a voice teacher in the house next door is the challenge now facing you. It began happening to

Uncle Verlon last spring. He has always had excellent hearing, age barely making a dent in his acuity. He works as a night guard in a downtown office building.

Uncle Verlon's neighbors come in all shapes and sizes and ages, including the singer who lives alone. With all the windows wide open, the accompaniment always comes from the radio or records. Uncle Verlon understands that. What puzzles him is the television set turned up loud in the same house while the lady is singing along with the recordings. Possibly, the lady is shy and does not want people to know who is singing. But surely then she would keep the windows closed?

Regardless, Uncle Verlon cannot tolerate the resulting discord when he is trying to sleep. For the first time in his life, he requires hearing assistance--a good pair of ear plugs, but they are not comfortable to wear.

Dogfights, excitable children, lawn mowers or trumpet players may need a solution so you can sleep when the whole world wants you awake. Assuredly, you are not alone in your great need for quiet and comfort. Our civilized world is still geared to about that 9 to 5 routine. But it would fall apart if there were no one awake during those other hours to protect and process, to serve and care.

Maybe the day will soon come that more people living on a standard schedule will realize and appreciate the importance of their night counterparts and show more consideration. Until then, it's a cliché that "Someone has to do it" but . . . someone does. If that person is you, eventually you will find a way to sleep during the day.

In our case, our neighbors' noise level became so overwhelming that we had to move to save my husband's physical health and my sanity. Our next location, investigated during evenings and weekends, had lawnmowers, cats and dogs, a few nearby children, but no teenagers, no minibikes, no trombone players and no retired people with workshops. Instead, our non-Anglo neighbors across the street kept me awake with their gleeful, late-night parties. It was the best compromise we could find.

# # #

Bootlegged Books

Bootleggers. The word conjures up images of moonshine stills in the hills of Kentucky and North Carolina, where distillers and imbibers alike had their own secret code words to protect themselves from the law and its agents.

Then appear scenes of Cornish smugglers, long cadenced in one's heart from childhood recitations of Rudyard Kipling's 1906 *A Smuggler's Song* (about Sussex smugglers):

"Five and twenty ponies trotting through the dark –

Brandy for the Parson.

'Baccy for the Clerk;"

Today's smugglers and bootleggers are bereft of even the redeeming attributes of the smugglers who brought a child "a dainty doll, all the way from France" for having minded to her own, child's business, not theirs.

Always, bootlegging has involved illegal activities of some sort: items produced or transported without payment of customs duties, legal fees, licenses or royalties—even bootlegged Bibles taken into Communist or Islamic lands where people often ache for them. But bootlegged books for a general reading audience? Yes!

First, during 2002 "Harry Potter-Book V," was created, produced and sold in China. As reported on the BBC's website, *Harry Potter and Leopard Walk Up to Dragon* sold fast in Beijing street markets for one pound sterling (1.5 Euros). Not only had the anonymous Chinese author turned HP into a fat, hairy dwarf without magical powers in the book, but he had used J. K. Rowling's name and photograph on the cover. Rowling's agent was not amused, yet it's hard to imagine that legal steps can be successfully pursued, since thieves seldom recognize international law, and China's attitude toward the rights of others is not unknown.

Second, many members of PMA (Publishers

Marketing Association), now IBPA (Independent Book Publishers Association) exhibited in PMA's co-op booth at the Frankfurt Bookfair, October 9-14, 2002. By November 8, I had been contacted by a publisher who first wished to purchase English rights to *Discoveries: A Journey Through Life* for Malaysian distribution. He referenced a director of PMA, implying that he had her approval. The contract had problems, such as an unspecified advance that would have come out to a total of perhaps 75 cents, with no projected print run.

It may be normal for publishers in less affluent societies to peddle books door-to-door and not have them in bookstores at all, but the more I studied that e-mail, the smellier it became. I contacted PMA and was advised to proceed with great caution, since the individual had contacted everyone in PMA's Frankfurt catalog! No publisher can take on hundreds of books at once with the intent to pass honest royalties on to the authors. This person only seemed bent on obtaining a free copy of many books from unsuspecting authors or publishers to make bootlegged copies for illegal distribution.

Third, books are a luxury item in Third World countries, including the islands of the sea. In fact, any item of value is stolen from their mail, never reaching the addressee. It is sad enough that schoolchildren in such countries are trying to learn without books. It's surprising that a G-rated book I wrote could become a valuable black market commodity among the grown-ups!

# # #

www.ingramcontent.com/pod-product-compliance
Lightning Source LLC
Chambersburg PA
CBHW070519130626
46555CB00003B/1284